Zane the Rodeo Zebra
by Lori Kaiser

Another great book in the Xavier Series!

Published by
Fleming Publishing
18204 Cooper Road
Conroe, TX 77302
281-635-2395

www.flemingpublishing.com

© Copyright, 2010 by Fleming Publishing. All Rights Reserved. No portion of this book may be reproduced, stored in a retrieval system, or transmitted, in any form or by any means, electronic, mechanical, photocopying, recording, or otherwise without prior written permission from publisher.
Printed in the United States of America
ISBN 978-0-9778968-7-5

To the Zybach family and their son, Zane:
The kid who can do anything.

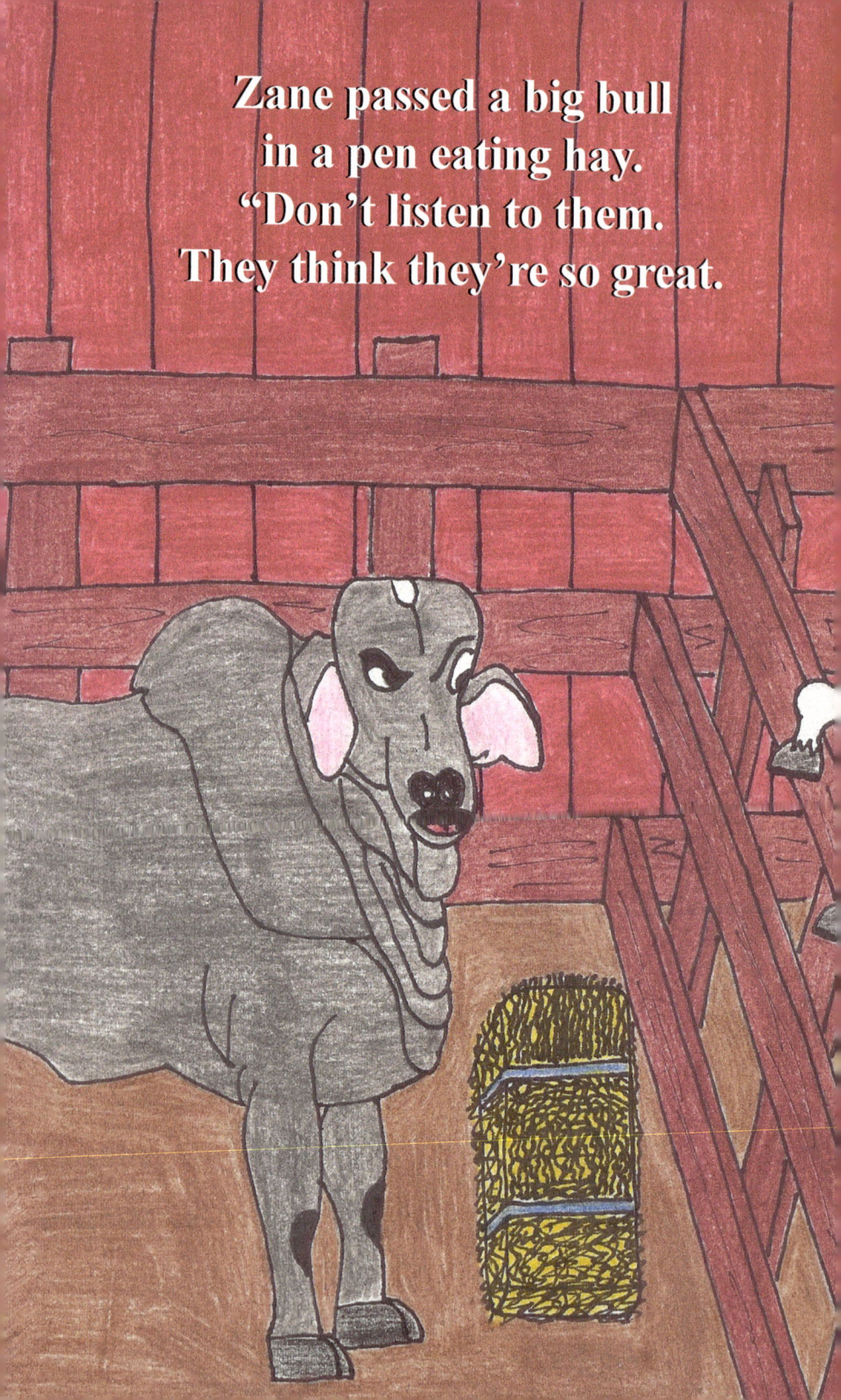

He knew who he was
and was proud of his stripes.
Now he's the one
the cowboys like.

www.ingramcontent.com/pod-product-compliance
Lightning Source LLC
Chambersburg PA
CBHW042045290426
44109CB00001B/38